Bob Heman

A Sky Obscured by Bicycles

SurVision Books

First published in 2025 by
SurVision Books
Dublin, Ireland
Reggio di Calabria, Italy
www.survisionmagazine.com

Copyright © Bob Heman, 2025

Cover image: "a sky obscured by bicycles" by Bob Heman
Cover image © Bob Heman, 2025

Design © SurVision Books, 2025

ISBN: 978-1-912963-60-7

This book is in copyright. No part of this publication may be reproduced, stored in a retrieval system, or transmitted in any form or by any means without the prior permission in writing from the publisher.

Acknowledgments

Grateful acknowledgment is made to the editors of the following, in which some of these poems, or versions of them, originally appeared:

First Literary Review–East, Fixed & Free Quarterly, Home Planet News online, Indefinite Space, Muddy River Poetry Review, NOON: journal of the short poem, Unlikely Stories, and in the anthologies *The Arcade of Scribes* and *Contemporary Tangential Surrealist Poetry,* as well as in the annual *Brevitas* anthologies, the annual *Brownstone Poets Anthology,* and the annual *Riverside Poets Anthology.*

"Rumors" was first published as *Swoopcard 20* by *Fell Swoop.*
"Traces" first appeared on Craig Czury's blog, *Old School School.*

For Cindy, my close friend and collaborator.

CONTENTS

In	5
The Idea	6
Inventory	7
The Story Of	8
Process	9
Strategy	10
Compass	11
Education	12
Direction	13
Were	14
Repetition	15
Instructions	16
Weapons	17
Performance	18
One Becomes	19
Ascent	20
The Distance	21
Rumors	22
Distance	23
Blueprint	24
What They Remember	25
Water	26
A War	27
The Part	28
The War	29
Remember	30
The Seen	31
The House	32
Laughing	33
Startled	34
Color	35
Drift	36
That	37
Traces	38
Thread	39
Dimensions	40
Night	41
Music	42

In

in the dark place
in the forest
where the stars, etc.

where the man
is deeper than
and the water is
broken into trees

The Idea

the idea of
or an outline

the words extra
or no longer
a description of

the dimensions those
of a rhino or giraffe
or a man who
has been inflated

the story starting
in this way

Inventory

An electrical device to move the horizon closer.
Three tiles to repair the damaged wall.
A woman who resembles but is not the same as.
A pair of camels that must be counted again.
A word that can have many different meanings.
Some light that changes the perspective.

The Story Of

the story of
was a man
replaced with numbers

a line drawn
where no line
had been before

a map folded
so that it
all made sense

Process

couldn't
remember
what it
was called
so called it
by a different
that then
became
its name

Strategy

the shoes
an explanation
for the chair
or window
but only after
the train
has arrived

Compass

The affectations of dining.

The wearing of nonfunctional garments.

The use of artificial speech patterns.

Journeys taken with no purpose.

Education

the difference
between the
farm and
the shipyard
between the
centipede and
the gopher
between the
kite and
the diving bell

Direction

the usual
playing pieces
men women
dogs cats

the sun
or moon
the ocean
or mountain

the sky
that approaches
before they
can leave

Were

"were we different?"

the light remembered
as something else

the man leaning
against the sky

the whole town
only a construct

Repetition

the story of
another repetition
of the clouds
in the pond
of the door
to the garden
of the man
and the woman
who found
each other at last

Instructions

Look to see who raises the shade.
Follow the stream to its source.
Use the word "thus" as frequently as possible.
Count the boats that are left in the harbor.
Hide the gun before the vicar arrives.
Mend the flags that had been buried.
Allow your hands to explore the tree.
Ask the woman to explain her wounds.
Learn how the motor should be used.
Always leave the lights on.

Weapons

the weapons they brought
from the other place:

the teddy bear
the woman's face
the tire made of glass

Performance

was only what
but never repeated
the applause different
when it was expected
the room larger
once we learned to listen
the distance then
only an assumption

One Becomes

one becomes only
what is necessary

the ocean sometimes
or a frog
or door

the man painted
so that he resembles

the woman a shadow
if she is even seen

the machine
never turned on

Ascent

one can climb
to dispel the laughter
to add the ocean
to the ceiling
and the birds
to the trembling gown
she slides into
inside her dreams

The Distance

the distance between
or the man running
his own voice chasing him
until he is able

the surface of
only where the sea
seems to begin or end

his name given to him then

Rumors

The distance a code that only resembled.

The words gathering behind the easiest explanation.

He was a mannequin first and then he was not.

He was only the way the woman's story was told.

What came next a kind of response.

The colors easier then.

Distance

the hand more distant
than the arm can reach

the river deeper than the air

each word a woman
surprised at her own cleverness

the moon always
a kind of explanation

Blueprint

the blueprint
for the fire
only a dog
asleep on the hill

the definition of
the only explanation
we can see

we are rounder then
but without the movement
that makes us necessary

What They Remember

what they remember
was only sometimes
a door only
sometimes a woman
or giraffe on fire
only sometimes the
steps taken to retrieve
the words spoken
only sometimes a color
repeated too often
that was theirs alone

Water

the water colder
than the night

she bathes in it
the way the saints

her own voice
never quite a prayer

A War

a far more dangerous war
approaches us and threatens
both our sleep and love
& threatens as well
what we expect to find
once the door is opened
and we can no longer dream

The Part

the part we are not
meant to see
when the mechanisms
that cause it
are revealed
and our "wow"
changes into an "oh"

The War

sometimes the war approaches
and the flowers stop growing
and the bears stop singing
and where the river should be
there are only arrows
we are supposed to follow
as if there was some place to go

Remember

They remember the room differently.

The zebras were only one way of explaining it.

Each word spoken a sapling not yet firmly rooted.

What they understood was never a forest.

There was always a knock on the door.

The Seen

one is able to see
what can be seen
the difference always
how it is interpreted
the man or woman
also animals that have
sprung from the forest
their calls confused
with a language
the bears or birds
might use
if suddenly startled

The House

the same house
is a different house
the trees different
the sky different
the words spoken
describing what it is not
even though it
continues to resemble
what it always was

Laughing

they laugh at the cook
because he is not a bear
and at the priest
because he is not a tree
they laugh at the dawn
because it arrives too late
and at the sea
because it cannot be described
they understand that adjectives
are the wrong kind of solution
and that the verbs will only arrive
once it is too late
each man who enters
an exception to the rule of pairs

Startled

startled by the light
inside the woman
inside the zebra
inside the maple trees

startled by the light
the river carries
to the silo
to the barn that holds
the frozen bears
to the orchard where
the apples grow too large

startled by the light
that was chosen
instead of darkness

Color

color added to the map
to the sky to the river
to the woman resting
beneath the multi-colored trees
her words with no way
to describe what she sees

Drift

one hesitates
to use the words
they were given

in their place
the buildings
grow larger

and the masks
the cattle wore
are removed

That

that becomes a river
or some earth that is burning
or a sky obscured by bicycles
that describes the shadows
cast by the giraffes
before they are swallowed
by the barn

Traces

The trees larger than required.

The map showing more than was necessary.

The food allowed never enough.

The gun only sometimes a weapon.

Thread

a flock of giraffes
pasted onto the horizon
wandering beneath the gaze
of the magnifying glass
becoming what is named
that cannot be escaped

Dimensions

The flower not an excuse.

The road not an explanation.

Each animal a way of counting.

The woman only a replica.

The machine no more than a sound.

Night

plays with the night

with the way
it touches the children
before they are ready

inside it the animals
grow larger and more fierce

inside it even gentle words
become a threat

Music

music the
only system
he understands

it resembles
the giraffes
or the
shadows cast
by the clouds

www.ingramcontent.com/pod-product-compliance
Lightning Source LLC
Chambersburg PA
CBHW061307040426
42444CB00010B/2552